Worry Habits

A Story to Help Children Better
Understand and Manage OCD

Copyright © 2023 Corbett Shwom

Copyright © 2023 Corbett Shwom.

ISBN-13: 979-8-218-12921-7

All rights reserved. This book or any portion thereof may not be reproduced or used in any manner whatsoever without the express written permission of the author except for the use of brief quotations in a book review.

The contents of this book is not an attempt to practice medicine or give specific medical advice concerning mental health. The book is intended to be informational and a motivational tool that may help the reader with their OCD. It is not intended to be a substitute for professional advice, diagnosis, or treatment. Always seek the advice of a mental health professional or other qualified health provider with any questions you may have regarding OCD.

Published by Worry House Press.
First Edition
Printed in the United States of America.

www.corbettshwom.com

This book is dedicated to each Little C out there. Just know that OCD doesn't define you, it's the bravery with which you face each day that does!

You see, Little C needed everything to be exactly the way it had to be.

He had to touch the light four times at night,
1-2-3-4.

Did it feel right? Not sure.
So he touched it some more.

Was the picture straight on the wall?
He would move it left, move it right.

Did it feel right?
Not sure.

He would say out loud,
I did this, I touched that, I made a mess,
I must confess. It's okay, right?

Over and over, he would say,
"I like girls" throughout the day.

Something if he didn't say,
that would make him gay.

He would wash his hands, clean the floor,
even though both felt like such a chore.

Did it feel right? Not sure.
So he would wash and clean some more.

What was it that they said
as he played the conversation
over and over in his head?

As he would lie in bed,
the day played through his head.

Did I do it right? Did I do it wrong?
Do I belong? Do you want to be friends?
They said it depends.

Did I say good night?
Did I hug my mom tight?

Oh no! Will she be all right?
My chest feels tight.

One day, Little C,
being as brave as he could be,
asked his mother,

"Why do I need to do things until it feels right?
Why do I feel scared and too afraid to fight?"

"I don't know why, dear," she said. "But we should go ask your doctor instead.

Thank you for having the courage to let me know. Now, off to the doctor we go."

What a surprise to Little C,
when it came to be,
that he had something called OCD.

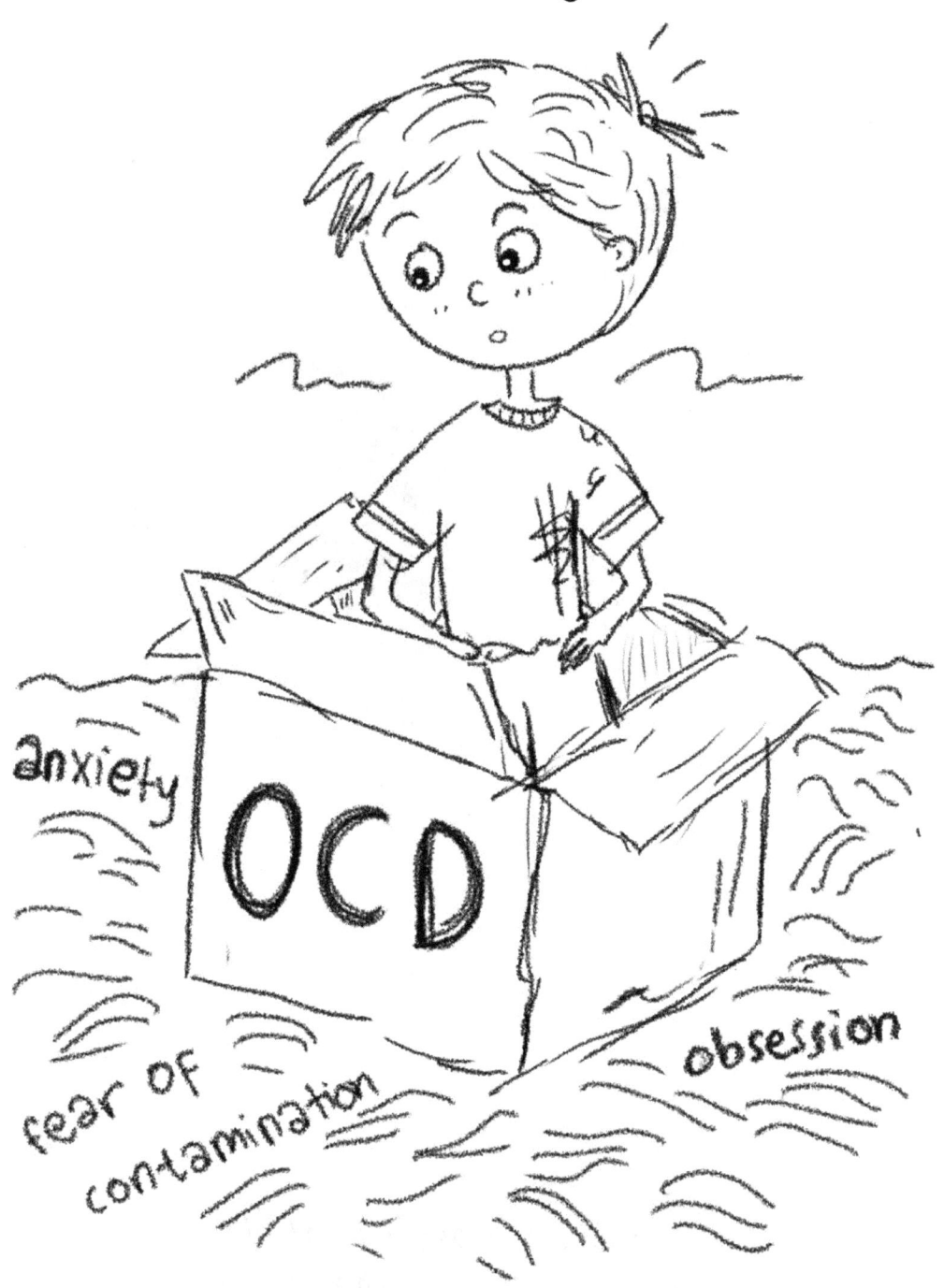

It starts with a worry that doesn't make you feel right. It makes you feel scared and too afraid to fight.

So you perform a task,
thinking this will make everything okay,
that this will help make the worry go away.

You repeat the task until it feels right,
whether it's the morning, afternoon, or night.

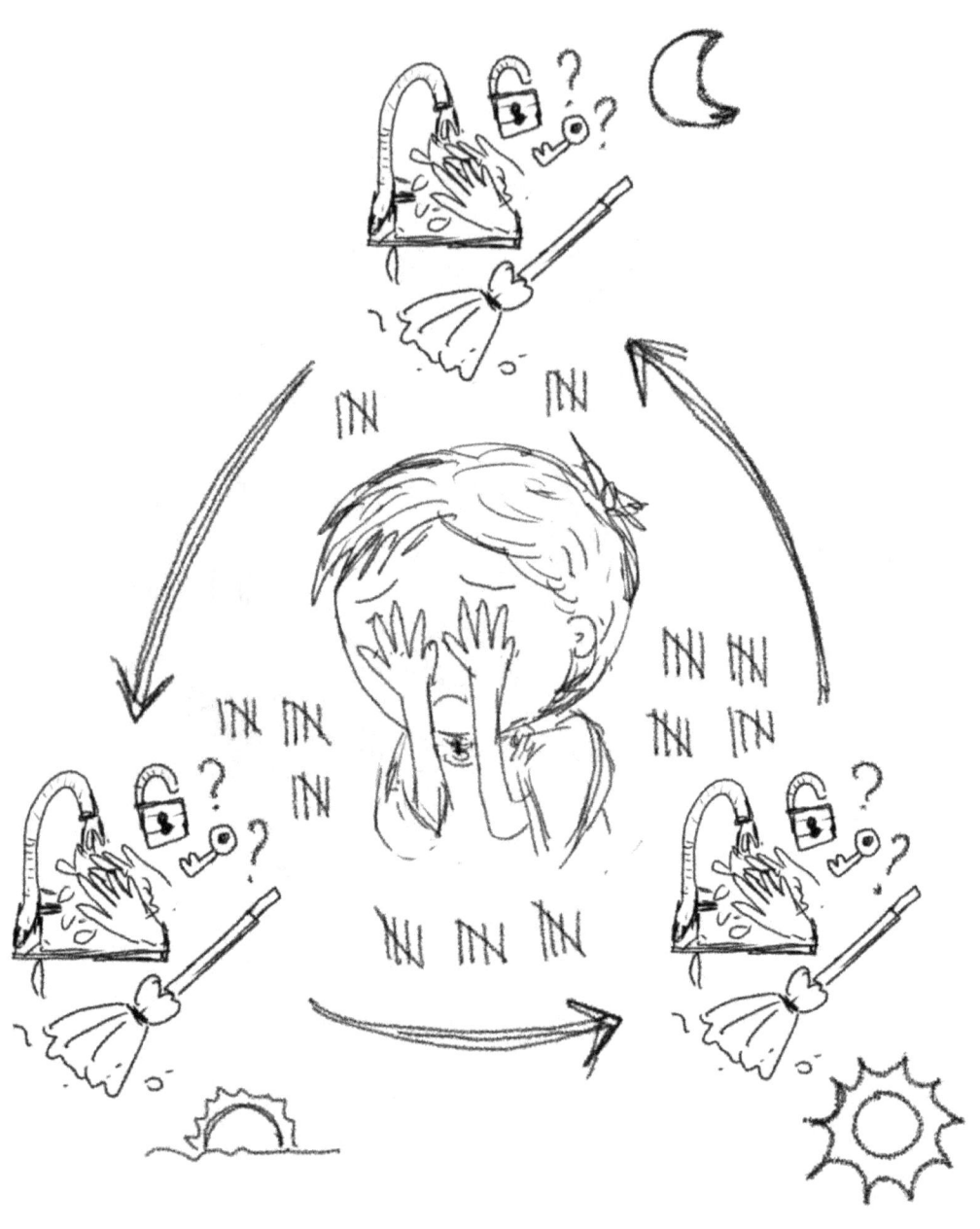

And all these tasks that you just can't quit,
turn into a worry habit.

But the worry is too strong
and gets in the way.
As you repeat the habit, it causes you delay.

Even worse, it makes you stay, preventing
you from doing things like going out to play.

With the help of his doctor and support from his parents,

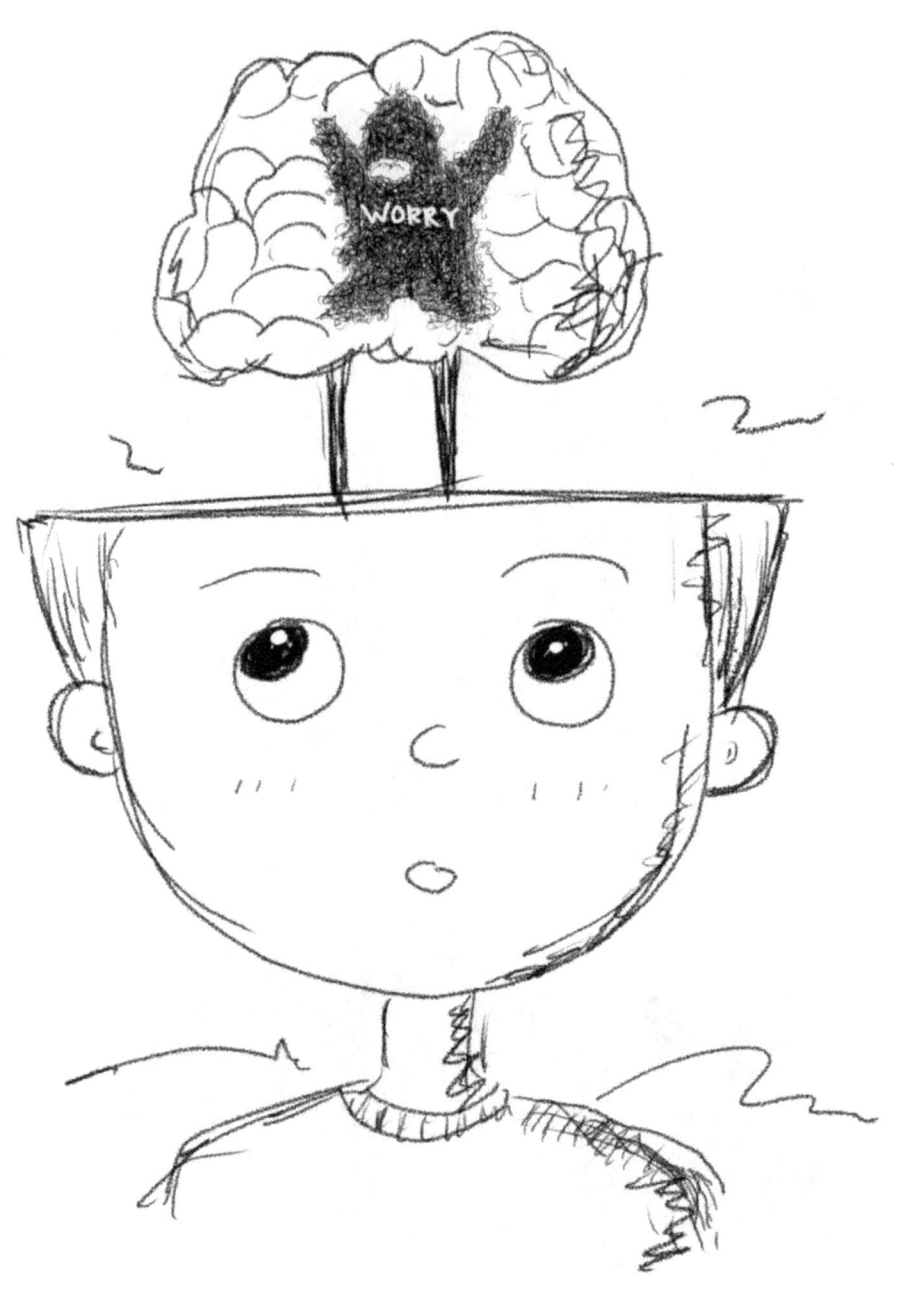

Little C started to learn that his worry thoughts were **just thoughts** and **nothing more.**

And that just because he thought them, it didn't make them true. He remembered his doctor telling him,

"Your brain isn't magic, so **don't let the thoughts upset you.**"

And to "let the worry thoughts come and go, if you give them **no attention**, there will be **no show**."

He also learned to say to the worry thoughts that day, "You are **not real**, so go away! Only happy thoughts can stay.

You can't hurt me or the ones I love," as he gave the worry thoughts a shove.

And rather than having feelings of doom and dread, take several **deep breaths** instead.

He remembered his doctor telling him to "**be strong** like a soldier and do something called exposure."

This is when you **face your worries**,
taking no action,
knowing that what you fear will not happen.

And the more he **confronted** his worries this way, the more it helped make the fear of them **go away**.

It wasn't easy for Little C, and he didn't always feel right, but he wasn't as scared because he was learning to **fight**.

He worked hard every day to not let his worries get in the way, taking no action, knowing **nothing bad was going to happen.**

Little C was **no longer** giving his OCD any satisfaction.

Author's Note

OCD–obsessive compulsive disorder–is not something that just goes away, so be kind and patient with yourself every day.
Continue to use the tools you are learning and seek the right help along the way, and I promise you, you'll have brighter days.

How do I know? Well, you see, Little C was me. ♥

Other Titles by Corbett Shwom

Worry Thoughts
A Story to Help Children Manage Worries and Anxious Thoughts

Worry Shy
A Story to Help Children Better Understand and Manage Social Anxiety

Be It! Act It!
An Alphabet of Positive Emotions and Feelings

Newsletter

Get notified about Little C updates and new book releases.

https://corbettshwom.com

www.ingramcontent.com/pod-product-compliance
Lightning Source LLC
Chambersburg PA
CBHW060622070426
42449CB00042B/2465